Nature Up Close

by Alice Boynton

LOOK! BOOKS™

Red Chair Press   Egremont, Massachusetts

Look! Books are produced and published by Red Chair Press:

Red Chair Press LLC   PO Box 333   South Egremont, MA 01258-0333

www.redchairpress.com

 FREE Educator Guides at www.redchairpress.com/free-resources

Publisher's Cataloging-In-Publication Data
Names: Boynton, Alice Benjamin.
Title: Nature up close / by Alice Boynton.

Description: Egremont, Massachusetts : Red Chair Press, [2019] | Series:
    Look! books. Look closely | Interest age level: 004-007. | Includes Now
    You Know fact-boxes, a glossary, and resources for additional reading.
    | Includes index. | Summary: "In Nature Up Close, young readers first
    view a butterfly wing, cactus spines, the leaves of a Venus flytrap,
    and the shell of an armadillo. Then readers see each plant and animal
    in its natural environment and learn how these features contribute to
    its survival."--Provided by publisher.

Identifiers: ISBN 9781634406666 (library hardcover) | ISBN 9781634406703
    (paperback) | ISBN 9781634406741 (ebook)

Subjects: LCSH: Morphology (Animals)--Juvenile literature. | Animals--
    Adaptation--Juvenile literature. | CYAC: Morphology (Animals) |
    Animals--Adaptation.

Classification: LCC QL799.3 .B69 2019 (print) | LCC QL799.3 (ebook) | DDC
    591.4/1 [E]--dc23

LCCN: 2018955656

Photo credits: cover, pp. 4–5, 6–7, 8–9, 10–11, 12–17, 21, 22, 24 iStock;
pp. 1, 6, 10, 18–20 Shutterstock.

Printed in United States of America

0519 1P CGF19

Table of Contents

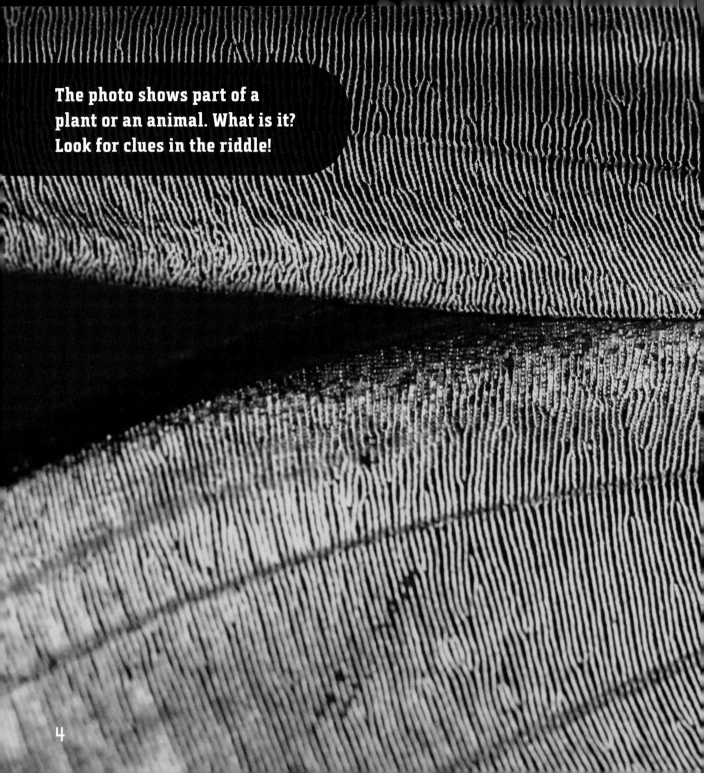

The photo shows part of a plant or an animal. What is it? Look for clues in the riddle!

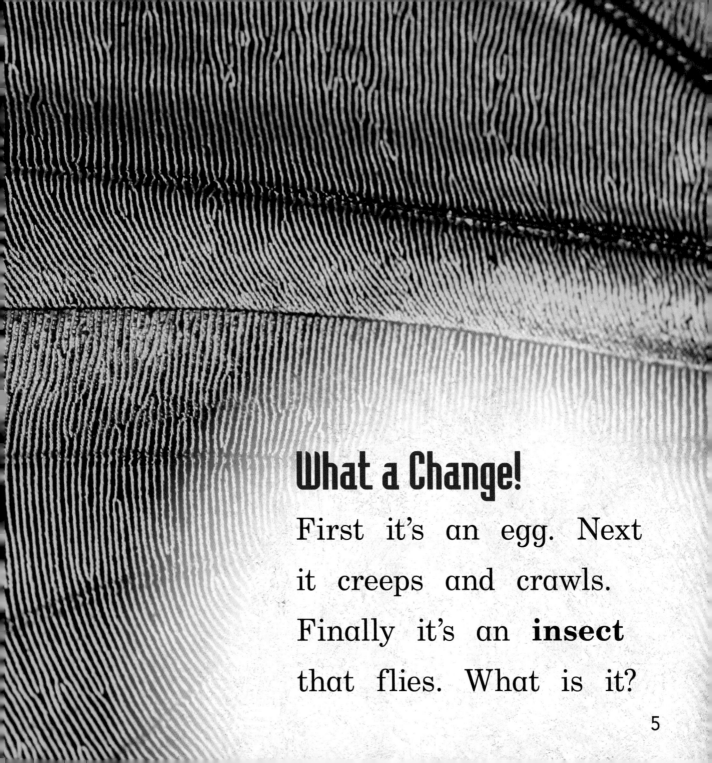

What a Change!

First it's an egg. Next it creeps and crawls. Finally it's an **insect** that flies. What is it?

It's a butterfly. It lives in the **rain forest**. Its wings are bright blue on top, but brown underneath. When the butterfly lands, it folds its wings. They look like leaves. Hungry birds are fooled!

Blue Morpho butterfly

Desert Giant

It grows tall in
the hot sun. It has
arms reaching up
and up. But don't
get too close. You
might get stuck.
Ouch! What is it?

It's a cactus. It grows in the **desert**. Very little rain falls there. So how does the plant get enough water to stay alive? It stores rain in its big stem.

See those holes? Birds made them. Birds move in, birds move out. It's a cactus hotel!

GOOD to KNOW

Saguaro cactus

Roly-Poly

This animal looks like it's wearing armor. But don't be fooled. It's not a knight. What is it?

It's an armadillo.
It looks **fierce**. But
it's not. If there is
danger, it curls up
into a ball. Its shell
protects it. An
armadillo has a long,
sticky tongue. Perfect
for lapping up ants
in their nests. *Slurp!*

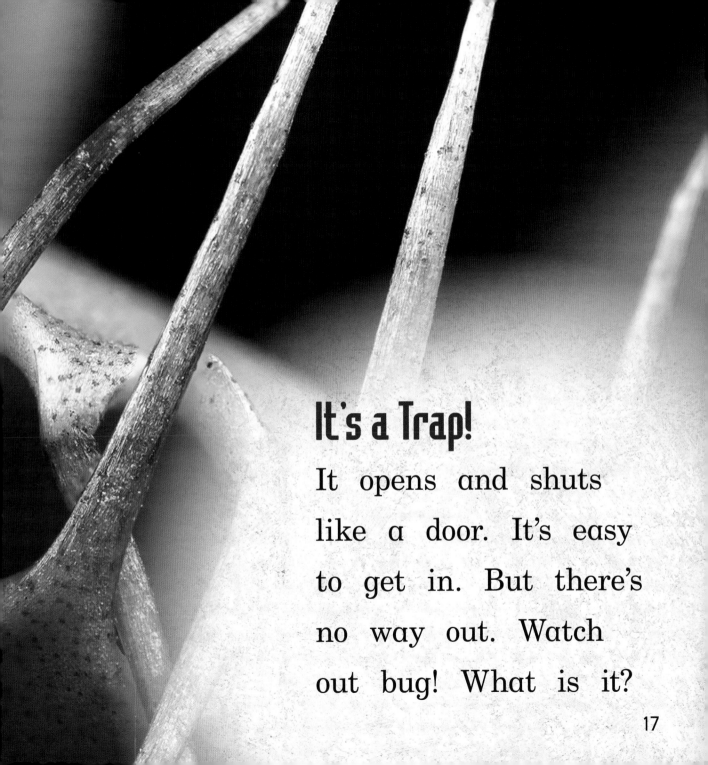

It's a Trap!

It opens and shuts
like a door. It's easy
to get in. But there's
no way out. Watch
out bug! What is it?

It's a Venus flytrap. Most plants get food from the **soil**. But this plant needs to eat bugs. If a fly lands on it, *SNAP!* The leaves shut. The fly is trapped. It's lunchtime for this plant!

GOOD to KNOW

The Venus flytrap makes juices. The juices break down the bug for the plant's food. It takes about a week. Then it's time to eat again.

A bee caught in
a Venus flytrap

Test Yourself!

What are these? Here's a clue. One is a plant. Two are animals. Look closely!

1

2

3

1 zebra

2 sunflower

3 seahorse

Words to Keep

desert: a hot, sandy place where very little rain falls

fierce: strong and brave

insect: an animal without a backbone that has six legs, such as a fly or spider

protects: keeps safe

rain forest: a place with many trees and animals, where it is hot and very rainy

soil: the part of the ground where plants grow

Learn More at the Library

Books (Check out these books to learn more.)

Guiberson, Brenda Z. Illustrated by Megan Lloyd. *Cactus Hotel* (Owlet Book). Henry Holt and Company, 1993.

Fowler, Allan. *Plants that Eat Animals* (Rookie Read-About Science). Children's Press, 2001.

Web sites (Ask an adult to show you these web sites.)

Armadillo San Diego Zoo
https://www.youtube.com/watch?v=r0e-tiKu2P4

Secret Life Of A Cactus—National Geographic Video
https://video.nationalgeographic.com/wild/secret-life-of-a-cactus

Springs Preserve Butterfly Habitat Facts: Blue Morpho
https://www.youtube.com/watch?v=hharKrtRFkk

Venus Flytraps: Jaws of Death – BBC One
https://www.youtube.com/watch?v=O7eQKSf0LmY

Index

About the Author

Alice Boynton has over 20 years of experience in the classroom. She has written many books on how to teach with nonfiction. She looks closely at nature around her at home in New York City.